marijuana today

Growing Career
Opportunities
in the Marijuana Industry

marijuana today

The Benefits of Medical Marijuana:
from Cancer to PTSD

Growing Career Opportunities
in the Marijuana Industry

Marijuana: Facts, Figures, & Opinions

Marijuana in Society

Marijuana's Harmful Effects on Youth

marijuana today

Growing Career
Opportunities
in the Marijuana Industry

Andrew Morkes

MASON CREST

Mason Crest
450 Parkway Drive, Suite D
Broomall, Pennsylvania 19008
(866) MCP-BOOK (toll-free)
www.masoncrest.com

First printing
9 8 7 6 5 4 3 2 1

ISBN (hardback) 978-1-4222-4104-2
ISBN (series) 978-1-4222-4103-5
ISBN (ebook) 978-1-4222-7692-1

Cataloging-in-Publication Data on file with the Library of Congress

Developed and Produced by National Highlights Inc.
Proofreader: Mika Jin
Interior and cover design: Yolanda Van Cooten
Production: Michelle Luke

QR CODES AND LINKS TO THIRD-PARTY CONTENT

contents

KEY ICONS TO LOOK FOR:

Words to understand: These words with their easy-to-understand definitions will increase the reader's understanding of the text while building vocabulary skills.

Sidebars: This boxed material within the main text allows readers to build knowledge, gain insights, explore possibilities, and broaden their perspectives by weaving together additional information to provide realistic and holistic perspectives.

Educational Videos: Readers can view videos by scanning our QR codes, providing them with additional educational content to supplement the text. Examples include news coverage, moments in history, speeches, iconic sports moments and much more!

Text-dependent questions: These questions send the reader back to the text for more careful attention to the evidence presented there.

Research projects: Readers are pointed toward areas of further inquiry connected to each chapter. Suggestions are provided for projects that encourage deeper research and analysis.

Series glossary of key terms: This back-of-the-book glossary contains terminology used throughout this series. Words found here increase the reader's ability to read and comprehend higher-level books and articles in this field.

Introduction

In the past decade, public opinion regarding cannabis legalization has begun to change around the world. A growing number of countries have legalized the medical use of cannabis to treat pain, nausea caused by cancer and other diseases, poor appetite and weight loss caused by chronic illnesses, muscle spasms caused by multiple sclerosis, seizure disorders, Crohn's disease, and other medical conditions. It is also being used to help fight the opioid abuse crisis and post-traumatic stress disorder (which is experienced by some military veterans; those who have been victims of natural disasters, serious accidents, terrorist incidents, or physical or sexual assault; and others). Countries that have legalized medical cannabis in recent years include the United States (in a majority of states), Canada, Australia, Spain, Portugal, Jamaica, Colombia, the Czech Republic, Switzerland, Romania, Germany, India, Israel, Macedonia, South Africa, and Uruguay.

A small but growing number of countries have also legalized or decriminalized the use of recreational cannabis by adults. (Decriminalization means reducing or getting rid of punishments for having and using small amounts of cannabis.) Recreational use of cannabis has been decriminalized in the United Kingdom, Ireland, France, Denmark, Italy, Spain, Czech Republic, and Germany, although it is still technically illegal. The Netherlands has long ignored recreational cannabis use, but has recently created stricter laws. In the United States, eight states have legalized recreational cannabis for adult use: Alaska, California, Colorado, Maine, Massachusetts, Nevada, Oregon, and Washington.

While the trend is toward the legalization of medical marijuana—and to a lesser extent, recreational marijuana—some countries still have very restrictive laws regarding the use of cannabis. These nations include China, France, Nigeria, Norway, Poland, Ukraine, the Philippines, Singapore, Japan, Vietnam, Malaysia, Indonesia,

South Korea, Thailand, Saudi Arabia, the United Arab Emirates, and Turkey, among other countries.

In countries where the use of medical and recreational marijuana is legal, a new industry has emerged, and profits are high. Legal marijuana sales in North America (U.S. and Canada) grew 30 percent in 2016, and totaled $6.7 billion, as reported by the cannabis industry research firm Arcview Market Research. The industry may earn $20.2 billion by 2021.

As the cannabis industry has grown, many new career opportunities have emerged in areas ranging from agriculture, scientific research, and marijuana dispensaries, to marketing, security, information technology, transportation, lobbying, and even tourism. Jobs are available around the world in countries that have legalized medical cannabis, recreational cannabis, or both. The U.S. cannabis industry alone employs 165,000 to 230,000 workers. This number could more than double in the next three to five years. *Marijuana Business Daily* predicts that Canada could add 150,000 new marijuana positions over the next several years. Here are some reasons why a career in the marijuana industry is a good idea.

Good pay. Salaries for marijuana industry professionals are good overall—especially for those who work in research, own or manage successful cannabis dispensaries, or offer legal and consulting services to cannabis businesses. For example, dispensary owners can earn $100,000 to $1 million, or upwards of six figure salaries or more depending on the size of their facility and the number of clients served. Dispensary managers earn salaries that range from $70,000 to $100,000 or more. Some careers (such as budtenders and bud trimmers) pay lower salaries, but workers in these jobs can advance to positions that offer better pay.

Rewarding work environment and many career options. The marijuana industry offers many types of work environments, including farms, growing facilities, cannabis dispensaries, laboratories, and offices (for marketing, information technology, legal services and other workers).

Jobs can't be offshored. Many marijuana industry careers involve hands-on work at farms, dispensaries, and laboratories that require the worker to be on-site to do his or her job. As a result, there is no chance that your position will be offshored to a foreign country.

Job opportunities are available in most U.S. states and more than twenty-five other countries. Although you will not find a marijuana-related job in every state or country, there are many places that offer jobs. If you want to break into the industry, you can move to states or countries where the use of cannabis is legal.

By the time you finish reading this book, you'll learn about more than forty careers in the marijuana industry, the educational paths you can take to prepare for the field, key skills for successful marijuana workers, typical salaries, methods of career exploration, reasons why the marijuana industry is expected to continue to grow, and much more. But you don't need to select a career right now. Check out the careers in this book to learn more. If a few careers seem especially interesting, try to learn more by talking to people in the field, watching videos of people in these jobs (YouTube is a good resource), and visiting the websites of marijuana industry associations. Good luck with your career exploration!

Marijuana is sometimes grown via hydroponic cultivation, in the way these vegetables are being grown.

words to understand

cloning: The scientific process of creating a genetically identical cutting (or clipping) from a parent strain of a cannabis plant.

curing: A process that is undertaken after marijuana is dried to increase the quality of the product.

irrigation: Bringing water to plants through artificial means such as pipes and misters.

mother plant: The marijuana plant that is the most productive and produces the desired attributes. Marijuana farmers try to keep these plants healthy for a long time to ensure that they can continue to take clippings from it to grow new plants. Also known as a **parent plant.**

yield: The final amount of an agricultural or industrial product after harvest or production is completed.

chapter 1

Careers in Agriculture, Growing, & Harvesting in the Marijuana Industry

Do you enjoy nature and growing things? Are you okay with getting dirty and working hard? If you answered yes to these questions, a career as a marijuana grower, or farmer, might be in your future.

Marijuana farmers grow cannabis at traditional-style farms under the sun or in indoor facilities that use sophisticated grow light and **irrigation** systems. Some marijuana farmers do not even use soil to grow cannabis. Instead, they use hydroponic systems in which the plant's roots are placed in nutrient-filled water. Other marijuana farmers use aeroponic systems. In these systems, no soil is used and the roots are misted with nutrient-rich water.

Marijuana farmers sometimes grow cannabis in indoor facilities that use drip irrigation systems, such as the one pictured above that is being used to grow vegetables.

Some farmers grow hemp, a cannabis plant grown for its fiber and used to make rope, textiles, paper, and many other products. It is also used to make non-psychoactive hemp oil (known as cannabidiol, or CBD). The use of CBD has reduced seizures in some patients with severe epilepsy as well as reduced the negative effects of other diseases and disorders. The growth of hemp is allowed on a state-by-state basis in the United States, and it is strictly regulated. It is also legal to grow industrial hemp in some countries such as China, France, Australia, and Canada.

Learn about the six main components of a female cannabis plant:

While it may seem like you could just get a couple of marijuana plants and start farming, it takes a lot more than that to be successful in the marijuana industry. Marijuana farmers must answer hundreds of questions before they are able to start farming. They include:

- Is it legal to grow marijuana in my state or country? If so, what type of marijuana farming is allowed?
- Will I grow my crop indoors or outdoors?
- How big will my grow area be? How many plants should I grow in this area?

Did You Know?

As of 2017, twenty-nine U.S. states permitted the use of medical cannabis, and Guam, Puerto Rico, and the District of Columbia had passed similar laws. Australia, Argentina, Chile, Israel, and more than twenty European countries had legalized medical cannabis as well.

Marijuana plants are dried in preparation for trimming and eventual sale.

- What types of marijuana strains will I plant? Which will be most successful in the climate where I live (or in outdoor farming)?
- What type of marijuana market will I serve: medical, recreational, or both?
- What type of soil should I use?
- Should I use organic or conventional fertilizer?
- If I farm indoors, should I grow my plants in the soil, hydroponically, or aeroponically?
- How will I fight animal and bug pests and protect my crops from harsh weather?
- What type of automated fertilization or irrigation systems should I use?
- How many people should I employ?
- Do I have money to start my business and keep it going?
- Who are my competitors? Will it be hard to break into the industry?
- What type of license do I need to get from the government to do this?

Many aspiring marijuana farmers either have a lot of experience working at marijuana farms or grow facilities, or they hire a *grow master* to help. These skilled professionals—who are also known as *lead growers*—have a lot of experience managing the operations of a commercial-scale farm or indoor grow facility. They know everything (or nearly everything) there is to know about growing marijuana. Job duties of grow masters include:

- Overseeing the design and construction of the grow operation
- Meeting with scientists and other experts to determine which strains they will grow

- Meeting with soil, fertilizer, and other suppliers
- Overseeing the various steps in the growing process: germinating, **cloning**, transplanting, and harvesting (including drying, **curing**, product storage, labelling and packaging, and transportation for sale)
- Managing planting schedules to create the highest **yield**, while also limiting production costs
- Maintaining a cultivation log that details every step in the growing process
- Providing general upkeep and care such as fertilizing, watering, protecting plants from weather damage and pests, monitoring for potential problems, and scheduling weeding, trellising (setting up wooden or metal support systems for plants as they grow), and other plant maintenance
- Ensuring that the **mother plant** stays healthy so that it can continue to be used to create new plants
- Coordinating crop rotation, which involves switching the types, or strains, of plants in a certain growing area to produce higher yields, enhance soil fertility, and create other benefits
- Consulting with specialists as needed to address issues with plant pests and diseases
- Hiring, training, and supervising staff, assistant managers, cultivation workers, and trimmers
- Building relationships with dispensary owners, managers, and budtenders
- Managing budgets
- Ordering supplies and equipment
- Staying up-to-date on legislation and other government regulations that may affect the business or the entire marijuana industry

A marijuana farmer discusses the rewards and challenges of owning a business:

Common Marijuana Bug Pests

Red spider mites suck the sap from the leaves; this kills the cannabis plant in a short time.

Thrips suck the chlorophyll from plant leaves, gradually killing the plant.

Aphids suck the sap from the plant and weaken it.

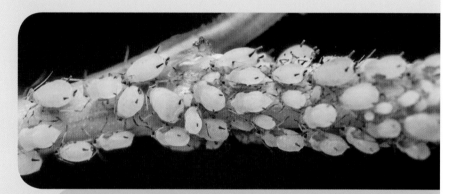

Aphids are among the most destructive insect pests of cultivated plants in temperate regions.

Leaf miners deposit eggs inside the leaves of the marijuana plant, and the hatched larvae "dig" tunnels that damage the plant.

Caterpillars are super-fast munchers that can destroy a marijuana plant in no time.

Whiteflies suck the sap from plants, weakening them.

Cochineals chew on plant material and leave droppings that contain a fungus that destroys plants.

Fungus gnats chew the fine root-hairs of plants, which reduces nutrient uptake and increases the chances of fungal infections in the roots.

A grow master who works in an indoor grow facility has specialized duties that include:

- Selecting irrigation and lighting systems
- Managing grow room environment control systems (temperature, humidity, air flow, etc.)
- Coordinating growth, irrigation, and plant relocation within the facility
- Managing fertilizer and chemical mixing and application

Most growers are on-call 24/7. If an indoor irrigation or lighting system breaks down in the middle of the night, the grow master must fix it. If an employee calls in sick, the grow master must take his or her place or find a last-minute replacement. This need to be available at all times can be tiring to those who have families or other personal interests.

The *assistant grow master*, also known as the *cultivation supervisor*, helps the grow master in his or her daily work and fills in for them when they are away from the job site.

Tour a marijua-na-growing operation in Kasilof, Alaska, and see bud trimmers at work:

Bud trimmers prepare marijuana plants for sale. They carefully cut buds from the large, leafy, flowery stalks to create a pleasing product. Both wet (recently picked) and dry plants are trimmed. Wet trimming usually happens over a few busy days. Finished flowers are then hung to dry or put on screens that offer good air

THC and CBD

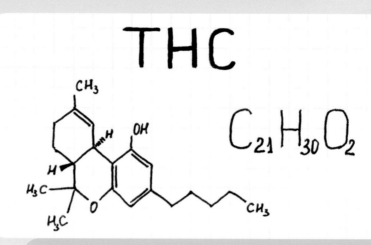

The chemical formula of Tetrahydrocannabinol, the chemical compound found in the marijuana plant that produces a feeling of euphoria and a psychoactive reaction, or "high."

Delta-9-tetrahydrocannabinol (THC) is a natural chemical compound found in the marijuana plant. It produces a feeling of euphoria and a psychoactive reaction, or "high," when marijuana is eaten or smoked.

Cannabidiol (CBD) is a chemical compound found in the cannabis plant that is non-psychoactive. It is known for its medical and pain relief properties.

circulation. Once the plants are dry (five to fifteen days), the trimmer checks for leaves that were missed the first time. There is not as much rush with dried plants. The trimmer cuts all or just a portion of the plant depending on production goals. Bud trimming is a good way to break into the industry, but this work can be repetitive and physically taxing on the hands and wrists. On the other hand, many trimmers view this job as a chance to earn reasonably good pay in a short time and "hang" with other trimmers in a busy, but relatively relaxed, setting. Some growers use cutting machines, which eliminate the need for bud trimmers.

Did You Know?

Recreational cannabis use is legal in eight U.S. states: Colorado, Washington, Oregon, Alaska, California, Massachusetts, Maine, and Nevada, as well as in Washington, D.C. The recreational use of cannabis has been decriminalized in France, Denmark, Italy, Spain, United Kingdom, Czech Republic, Ireland, and Germany, although it is still technically illegal. The Canadian government is currently in the process of legalizing cannabis for recreational purposes. Medical use is already legal there. In Latin America, Uruguay has legalized medical and recreational cannabis.

Processing workers prepare finished products for delivery to dispensaries. They roll marijuana cigarettes, weigh marijuana and seal it in bags or containers for sale, and attach labels that provide information on the THC and CBD content of each product.

Working on a farm is challenging. You'll spend much of your time outside in hot, humid, and sunny conditions. Your days start early—often before the sun rises. Many of your job duties will be repetitive, but necessary to create a successful crop. You'll frequently need to bend, reach, lift, pull, climb, and carry tools and equipment, so you'll need to be in excellent physical condition. On the other hand, many people enjoy the chance to be outdoors, work with their hands, and work in a non-corporate setting. They like playing a role in turning a tiny plant into a finished product that can help people with medical issues, or who just want to use marijuana for recreational purposes.

The marijuana industry offers a variety of career opportunities—from the agricultural side of the business, to careers in dispensaries, to those in sales and marketing.

A farmer harvests his marijuana crop.

text-dependent questions

1. What are five questions that aspiring marijuana farmers should ask themselves before they go into business?
2. What is a grow master?
3. What are some of the bugs that threaten the health of marijuana plants?

research project

Plant a vegetable garden in your backyard or on your deck. (If you don't have a deck or backyard, plant some herbs in a few pots on your kitchen windowsill.) Keep a journal that describes what you planted, when you planted it, and how it grew. Be sure to water and fertilize your plants, as needed. Track each plant's progress, and summarize what grew and what didn't at the end of the growing season. Write down why you think some plants grew well (e.g., quality soil, enough water, ample sun, etc.), and why some didn't (e.g., bugs, too much sun, too much water, etc.). Keep this information in mind when you plant a garden next spring.

Approximately 37,000 to 52,000 people work in medical and recreational dispensaries in the United States.

Liberty Farms
"Blueberry"
Use For: Pain Relief, Stress, Anxiety

NOT FOR SALE
Medical Use Only
ORS 475.300-475.346

Hybrid
Bry
Blueberry

words to understand

brand: A name and look given to a product or service by a company or other organization. Successful brands are well-known for being of high quality and having distinct designs or other attributes in their packaging (or as part of the actual product) that help them to stand out from those of competitors.

compliance: Following rules established by government agencies or other regulating bodies.

freelancer: A type of worker who does not work full-time for a company or organization, but who provides services as needed. Freelancers do not receive a regular salary, but are paid by the hour or project.

infuse: To cook or otherwise introduce ingredients, such as marijuana flowers, into food or drinks.

chapter 2

Other Career Paths in the Marijuana Industry

If you don't want to be a farmer or other type of agricultural worker, there are many other career paths in the marijuana industry. You can work in a marijuana dispensary, in a laboratory, in an office, or in many other settings. The following sections provide more information.

Careers at Dispensaries

A marijuana dispensary is a type of store where people can buy recreational or medical cannabis in U.S. states or other countries where it is legal to use marijuana. Dispensaries are tightly controlled by the government. Visitors must present personal identification, and medical marijuana patients need to present their doctor's recommendation for treatment with cannabis. The physical layouts of medical use and recreational use dispensaries are usually different.

A medical dispensary is often more like a doctor's office than a store. It will have a waiting room, where you will wait to meet one-on-one with the budtender, a specialist who knows everything there is to know about different types of marijuana (more on this career later).

A recreational dispensary is more like a regular store. People who want to buy marijuana wait in line, look at the various products, read menus listing the prices and types of cannabis (e.g., flower, concentrate, edible, topical, etc.), and then make their purchases at a counter.

The following paragraphs discuss some of the most-popular jobs in dispensaries.

The budtender is one of the best-known jobs in the marijuana industry. They work directly with customers at dispensaries. As a result, budtenders need excellent communication and customer-service skills, as well as detailed knowledge of the various strains of marijuana. They also need to know about the various types of marijuana products, such as marijuana that is smoked, as well as marijuana edibles, oils, concentrates, and vaporized products. They know how every product on the dispensary's shelves was created, where it was created, what it is used for, its potency, etc. The best budtenders know how to tell stories (from their own experience or those of others) about how a certain marijuana product improved their lives, helped address a medical problem, or simply provided a pleasant experience (recreational cannabis).

A budtender in a medical marijuana dispensary advises customers on what type of marijuana works best for a certain ailment, such as pain, nausea, lack of appetite, or seizures or other medical issues. They may spend up to twenty minutes asking the individual about his or her illness or injury, the side effects associated with it, and other questions that help them to determine what marijuana product to recommend. Budtenders either have direct experience using marijuana for medical reasons or they just know a lot about medical marijuana from studying articles about medical marijuana or from interacting with past customers. At a recreational cannabis dispensary, a budtender may not have as much time to spend with a client as a budtender at a medical cannabis dispensary does. There are often too many customers to spend more than a few minutes with each customer. Yet, they use their knowledge of marijuana products to suggest the right product for the customer.

Marijuana Dispensary Career Ladder

Dispensary Owner
Dispensary Manager
Budtender
Cashier
Receptionist

The name "budtender" is inspired by the career of "bartender," although their jobs are different in some respects. Unlike a bar, customers at a dispensary cannot use marijuana on site. So, the budtender does not use marijuana with customers—unlike a bartender, who may occasionally drink alcohol with customers. Non-service–related tasks for budtenders include preparing marijuana products for sale, restocking displays, and learning about new products.

Tour a medical marijuana dispensary, see what is required from a first-time visitor to a dispensary, and see a budtender at work:

Cashiers work closely with budtenders. This career is a good way to break into the field. They get to learn about marijuana as budtenders discuss various products with customers. They take payment from customers and bag their purchases. An experienced cashier can eventually become a budtender.

Receptionists greet customers when they enter the dispensary. They check customers' identification each time they enter the dispensary, and record each visit in a computer database. This is required by law. (At some dispensaries, *security officers* handle this task and make sure that both the staff and customers do not steal marijuana products.) Receptionists also answer questions from customers who are unfamiliar with the process of using a dispensary. The entry-level job of receptionist is a good way to learn about marijuana and what it takes to run a successful business. An experienced and motivated receptionist can advance to become a cashier and, eventually, a budtender.

Bud trimmers prepare marijuana plants for sale. They carefully cut buds from the large, leafy, flowery stalks to create a pleasing product. This is a good way to break into the industry, but the work can be messy and tedious. In addition to working at dispensaries, many bud trimmers work at marijuana farms and at indoor grow facilities.

Working as a marijuana delivery driver is a good way to break into the industry.

Delivery drivers work for medical marijuana dispensaries that have permission to deliver products to patients who are infirm or home-bound for other reasons. They also transport marijuana from farms and indoor grow facilities to dispensaries.

Cannabis dispensary owners supervise their staff, manage their company's finances, make sure their businesses are in **compliance** with government rules, order inventory and supplies, create advertising and marketing campaigns, hire and train employees, and do anything else necessary to keep their businesses running successfully. Some work as budtenders, interacting directly with customers. Some owners have a more hands-off approach to their businesses. They hire a dispensary manager to take care of all or some of these tasks, and only periodically visit the dispensary.

Like any type of business, dispensaries need support staff such as accountants, chief financial officers, and lawyers. A large dispensary might employ these workers full-time, while smaller ones might just hire them to work on a **freelance** basis.

The work environment for dispensary workers is good. Dispensaries are clean and well-lit. Most workers would describe their work environment as busy, but relaxed and friendly. There are a few drawbacks to this work. Budtenders and other dispensary workers may have to stand much of their workdays. Like any business, customers can be occasionally rude or demanding, but most are pleasant and happy for the opportunity to purchase cannabis for their medical or recreational needs.

Customer-facing jobs in dispensaries are a good fit for people who enjoy talking and interacting with others. Someone who is not outgoing would be most happy in behind-the-scenes jobs such as stock clerk, accountant, or bud trimmer.

Careers in Sales and Marketing

Many medical dispensaries employ marketing and sales specialists to design company logos, create print and online advertising, develop websites, and perform other tasks that help dispensaries get their names and **brands** out there. (In most medical marijuana markets, it is illegal to market or advertise dispensaries.) Sales and marketing specialists also perform the same duties for marijuana farms, growing facilities, and other marijuana-related businesses.

Web designers and *graphic designers* create print and digital marketing and sales materials. *Software designers* and *programmers* develop the information technology backbone of websites, apps, databases, and other technology used by marijuana businesses. One example of a marijuana app is Weedmaps.com, which helps users of legal marijuana find dispensaries, doctors, and other resources.

A wide range of career opportunities is available in the legal marijuana industry, including those in web design.

Cannabis sales representatives work for marijuana farms and growing facilities. They visit dispensaries and meet with owners, managers, and budtenders to try to convince them to sell the farm's or growing facility's products in the dispensary. They are experts in everything from the various strains and types of marijuana to government regulations. Other sales representatives are employed by soil producers, fertilizer manufacturers, and the manufacturers of growing equipment. They pitch their company's products to marijuana farmers.

Sales and marketing professionals work indoors in well-lit offices and dispensaries. They occasionally travel to trade conferences and other events. Cannabis sales representatives travel frequently between farms and growing facilities to dispensaries. In some areas, they may be on the road for several days at a time, meeting with the owners of dispensaries in a large geographic area.

Careers in Science

Although medical marijuana is legal in most U.S. states and in dozens of countries, not a lot of research has been conducted on its medical benefit and side effects. That's changing as governments allow more research and the public seeks more

A chemist tests cannabis extracts in a laboratory to explore its use for the treatment of a variety of medical conditions.

All About Laboratory Equipment

centrifuge: A machine with a rapidly rotating container that is used to separate liquids from solids or fluids of different densities.

gas chromatograph: A device that is used to separate substances that can be vaporized without decomposition or volatile compounds.

high-pressure liquid chromatograph: A device that is used to separate, identify, and quantify each component in a mixture.

mass spectrometer: A device that produces charged particles (ions) from chemical substances that are being analyzed. Magnetic and/or electric fields are used to determine the mass of the charged particles, which allows scientists to then determine the structure and elemental composition of the substance.

information on the benefits and drawbacks of using marijuana. There are many options in the marijuana industry for those who love science, conducting experiments, and finding answers to problems.

Geneticists, plant breeders, and *botanists* conduct research to develop strains of marijuana that help people with medical conditions or otherwise increase the potency of marijuana. They use gas chromatographs, high-pressure liquid chromatographs, centrifuges, mass spectrometers, and other technology to do their work.

Chemists study the structures and chemical properties of marijuana. They test marijuana products for potency (how high the levels of THC or CBD are) and to determine if high levels of pesticides, heavy metals (such as lead and mercury), or fungus (mold, etc.) are present. As discussed earlier, THC is a natural chemical compound in the cannabis plant that produces a feeling of euphoria and "high" when used; CBD is a chemical compound in cannabis that offers medical benefits and has pain relief properties, but does not create a "high" or feeling of euphoria.

Chemists and testing technicians are expected to be in strong demand as U.S. states and countries that have legalized marijuana seek to make marijuana as safe as possible for users.

Laboratory technicians assist chemists, botanists, geneticists, and other scientists. They conduct laboratory tests and present their findings to scientists; set up, maintain, calibrate, clean, and test laboratory equipment; and perform other support duties in the laboratory.

Extractors and *extraction technicians* are some of the most in-demand, highest-paid workers in the marijuana industry. They operate sophisticated CO_2 or butane extraction systems to extract cannabinoid oil from cannabis trimmings and/or flowers. These extracts often have high concentrations of CBD, which make them very effective for marijuana patients. This can be a dangerous job because extraction techniques involve high temperatures and high pressure. Extraction professionals must be very careful to avoid explosions and dangerous gas leaks as they do their work. Some U.S. states have only legalized the use of marijuana extracts, so job opportunities are especially good for extraction professionals in these states.

Laboratory managers oversee every aspect of their facility—from staffing and budgets, to quality assurance and equipment maintenance, to regulatory issues.

Scientists and technicians work in laboratories and research facilities. These settings are extremely clean and well-lit, and feature cutting-edge technology. Scientists and technicians must wear safety glasses and other protective gear when operating extraction systems or doing other tasks. Laboratories are staffed with people who are excited to be solving scientific problems and making new discoveries. Most scientists and technicians find this work rewarding and interesting.

Careers in Marijuana Edibles

Cannabis-**infused** foods and drinks are also very popular because they allow users to avoid the inhalation risks of smoking or vaping (inhaling the active ingredients of marijuana via vapors created by heating, but not burning, cannabis). Marijuana plant material or oil is infused into brownies, cookies, and other baked goods; chocolate-covered coffee beans; wine and beer; other food products; and even entire

A chocolate marijuana cake with marijuana butter is just one of many recipes an edibles chef can create.

meals. Ingestion causes the same euphoric or symptom-reducing effects of the smoked or vaped plant. Edibles typically have higher levels of THC than marijuana that is smoked or vaped. This is important for users of medical marijuana because edibles often provide a longer, more sustained "high"—and relief of nausea, pain, and insomnia.

An *edibles chef* is a skilled culinary professional who creates edible marijuana products. They make products by using hash oil or cannabutter made from ground marijuana flower, or the stems, leaves, and other parts of the cannabis plant. Other chefs use more complex processes, such as extraction, to make edibles. They operate sophisticated CO_2 or butane extraction systems to extract cannabinoid oil from cannabis trimmings and/or flowers. Because THC levels are higher in edibles, these chefs must be extremely careful that they create products with appropriate levels of THC, and that THC levels are listed on packaging.

Edibles products business owners sell their products to dispensaries, which then market them to customers.

The Arcview Group, a cannabis business research firm, notes that "concentrates and edibles are becoming customer favorites versus traditional smoking," and California reported $180 million in cannabis-infused edibles sales in 2016.

A successful edibles chef has artistic and creative ability; has completed coursework in chemistry, other sciences, and business; and has experience in commercial food production.

Working as an edibles chef is extremely rewarding because you get to work for yourself and build your business. You get to experiment with different foods and baking and production methods. And you get to make a living by doing something that you love.

Other Marijuana Industry Careers

One of the best aspects of the marijuana industry is that there are job opportunities for people with almost any interest and skill set. Here are some other popular careers in the marijuana industry:

Just like any other business, marijuana farms, grow facilities, and dispensaries need *accountants* to keep the books, manage cash (this is especially important because most banks do not allow marijuana growers to open accounts), be responsible for employee payroll, handle taxes, give financial advice, and perform other duties. Other financial positions include auditors, comptrollers, and chief financial officers.

Cannabis consultants are experts in one or more areas of the marijuana industry. They know a lot about marijuana—how to grow it, how to market and sell it, or how to comply with legal and regulatory issues. Some consultants have degrees in law, finance, or accounting. Others have experience as budtenders, grow masters, or marijuana business owners.

Marijuana lawyers provide advice to marijuana growers, dispensary owners, and other marijuana-related businesses about legal issues. They offer tips on setting up a business, complying with government rules, paying taxes, employment issues, and other areas. They are knowledgeable about intellectual property issues, which include patents for inventions, trademarks, and industrial designs, as well as copyrights for written products, videos, and related resources. Lawyers also represent marijuana businesses during legal proceedings.

Lobbyists work in Washington, D.C., U.S. state capitals, and the capitals of foreign countries. They know a lot about how government works, as well as a lot about the benefits of marijuana. They try to convince elected officials to pass laws that allow people to use marijuana for medical and recreational purposes.

Many people have misconceptions about marijuana. They think it is dangerous or have other negative opinions about it. *Marijuana educators* teach people about the benefits of medical marijuana. They bust misconceptions and provide hard facts and medical studies that show that medical marijuana is useful in reducing the side effects of many illnesses.

Marijuana legalization activists rally in Yonge-Dundas Square in Toronto, Canada.

Employment in the U.S. Marijuana Industry, 2016

Medical/Recreational Dispensaries: 37,000 to 52,000 workers

Ancillary Services (e.g., legal, marketing, etc.): 42,000 to 66,000 workers

Wholesale Cultivators: 15,000 to 27,000 workers

Infused Product Makers: 5,500 to 8,000 workers

Testing Labs: 990 to 1,300 workers

Source: Marijuana Factbook

Marijuana activists teach people about the benefits of medical and recreational marijuana. They organize legalization marches, write articles promoting marijuana, and use social media to spread positive information about marijuana.

Marijuana reporters cover marijuana-related news for newspapers, magazines, and websites. They interview people in the marijuana industry, and write stories about efforts to legalize or prohibit marijuana, the science of marijuana, medical breakthroughs, marijuana's effects on teens, and other topics. Some newspapers and magazines—such as the *Denver Post* in Colorado in the United States—even have special reporters that only cover the marijuana industry.

Marijuana reviewers assess the quality of various marijuana strains for publications such as *High Times* and websites such as Leafly and Wikileaf. This information is helpful to recreational users, but more importantly, to medical patients who need high THC or CBD strains.

Couriers and *drivers* transport marijuana from farms and grow facilities to dispensaries and laboratories. They also deliver medical marijuana products to infirm or homebound customers.

Marijuana tourism is an emerging sector as more cities, states, and countries that have legalized marijuana try to attract tourists from other states and countries. Opportunities are available at tourism offices, tour companies, tour guide publishing companies, and any other organization that promotes marijuana tourism.

As more states and countries legalize marijuana, there will be a growing need for *regulatory inspectors* to make sure that marijuana farms and dispensaries follow government rules, marijuana products meet quality and potency claims, and marijuana businesses follow tax, zoning, financial reporting, and other laws.

text-dependent questions

1. What type of workers use CO_2 or butane extraction systems?
2. What are some good career choices for people who like interacting with the public?
3. What do budtenders do?

research project

Create a marketing campaign for several types of fruits and vegetables in your garden. What would you say to convince people to buy your products?

words to understand

doctorate: A degree that is awarded to an individual who completes two or three additional years of education after earning a master's degree.

fringe benefits: A payment or non-financial benefit that is given to a worker in addition to salary. These consist of cash bonuses for good work, paid vacations and sick days, and health and life insurance.

internship: A formal or informal agreement in which a student receives on-the-job training from a company or other organization in exchange for pay, academic credit, or just the chance to obtain real-world experience (some internships are unpaid).

master's degree: An educational credential that is earned by completing two years of additional training after one earns a bachelor's degree.

union: An organization that seeks to gain better wages, benefits, and working conditions for its members. Also called a **labor union** or **trade union**.

chapter 3

Preparing for the Field and Making a Living

Educational Paths

Is a career in the marijuana industry in your future? If so, there are many ways to prepare. Some people train for the field by earning two- or four-year degrees from colleges and universities. Some even earn **master's degrees** or **doctorate degrees**. Marijuana industry workers have degrees in many majors. Others learn their skills by participating in informal and formal apprenticeships and **internships**, or by starting out in entry-level positions and learning their skills on the job. Others move into careers in the marijuana industry after working for several years in other industries.

Participating in agricultural programs while in school will provide good preparation if you want to become a cannabis farmer.

Taking High School Classes

Marijuana industry workers have a variety of skills and educational backgrounds. There are many high school classes that will be useful for those who want to enter the field. Here's an overview of popular courses and the careers that they will help students to prepare for (remember that many classes provide useful preparation for a variety of careers):

- **Biology, molecular biology, genetics, earth science, chemistry:** grow masters and other agricultural workers, research scientists, research technicians, extraction technicians
- **Mathematics:** almost any career, but especially scientists, grow masters, accountants and other financial professionals, business managers and owners
- **Accounting:** business managers and owners, chief financial officers, accountants, auditors
- **English, writing, and speech:** almost any career, but especially public relations specialists, lobbyists, social media professionals, and marijuana journalists and reviewers
- **Shop/vocational tech:** careers (such as carpenters, electricians, and heating and cooling technicians) that involve building and maintaining growing areas and facilities
- **Computer science, web design, information technology:** almost any career, but especially business owners and managers, web and graphic designers, software designers
- **Art and design:** web and graphic designers
- **Foreign languages:** useful for any worker who interacts daily with those who do not speak English as a first language and those who plan to pursue career opportunities in a foreign country

Some high schools offer specialized programs in agriculture, which will help you to prepare to become a grow master or work in other agricultural jobs. In such a program, you'll take typical courses such as English, biology, art, physical education, and geometry, but you'll also take specialized courses such as Agricultural Careers and Leadership, Introduction to Agricultural Science, Agricultural Career Pathways, and Environmental Science. At many schools, students get to select an agriculture-related pathway based on their interests. Examples of such pathways include:

- Agricultural Finance and Economics
- Agricultural Mechanics and Technology
- Animal Science
- Food Science and Technology
- Horticulture
- Biotechnology in Agriculture

In many programs, students develop their hands-on skills by planting, caring for, and harvesting a wide range of fruits and vegetables.

Participating in an Apprenticeship

Some people train for careers in the marijuana industry by participating in informal apprenticeships. These learning opportunities last from a few months to a year. Apprenticeships in the marijuana industry are not like the formal ones in the trades and other fields that are approved by government agencies and run by **unions**, professional associations, and other organizations. Their quality varies greatly. Some offer excellent preparation for careers, while others will teach you just enough to qualify for an entry-level position. Some unions that represent marijuana industry workers are lobbying politicians in states where marijuana is legal to create formal apprenticeship programs. (Lobbying is the process of trying to convince an elected or appointed official to support a position—such as protecting the environment, passing stronger gun control, laws, etc.)

Participating in an apprenticeship on a farm or in a plant nursery will provide a good introduction to work in the grow side of the cannabis industry.

Informal marijuana apprenticeships are available in many areas. For example, you can work as an apprentice at a marijuana dispensary, a bakery that sells marijuana edibles, a law office that provides legal services to marijuana business owners, or at a marijuana farm or indoor growing facility. Some employers might also refer to their apprenticeships as internships. An apprentice at a marijuana farm might have the following learning opportunities/work responsibilities:

- Propagation: seeding/planting/transplanting/cuttings
- Weed management
- Cultivation (breaking up and otherwise preparing the land to be planted)
- Irrigation (watering plants or managing indoor systems that deliver water to plants in indoor grow facilities)
- Harvesting
- Farm maintenance (repairing and maintaining equipment, tractors, and other farm gear)

Farm work is demanding. You'll need to be up before the sun rises, and work in hot weather under the blazing sun. The job is physically taxing, so you'll need to be in good shape. Other types of apprenticeships—such as those in a dispensary or at a law office—are located indoors and are far less physically challenging.

Attending College

Most people in the marijuana industry have two- or four-year degrees from colleges and universities. Some have master's degrees and doctorates. Marijuana industry workers have degrees in a wide range of areas. When you enroll in college, you'll be asked to choose a college major, a program of study that consists of classes in your field of interest. You'll take other classes, too. But many of your courses will focus on your specific interest—such as biology, marketing, business, accounting, or plant genetics (studying and working with the genes of plants to make healthier plants or ones that are larger or offer more fruits and vegetables).

Your major will vary greatly based on what type of career you're interested in. For example, if you want to work as a grow master, you should earn a degree in agriculture. If you want to own or manage a business, a two- or four-year degree in business management will be useful. If working as a research scientist is more your

Colleges and Universities That Offer Cannabis-Related Classes

University of California-Davis: Physiology of Cannabis

Oregon State University: Marijuana Policy in the 21st Century

Hofstra University: Business and Law of Marijuana

Ohio State University: Marijuana Law, Policy & Reform

University of Washington: Medicinal Cannabis and Chronic Pain

University of Vermont: Medical Cannabis and Pharmacology 200: Cannabis Past, Present, and Future

Harvard University: Tax Planning for Marijuana Dealers

University of Denver: Representing the Marijuana Client

thing, then you would major in plant biology, chemistry, or another science-related field. If you want to create websites and advertising materials for the marijuana industry, then you should study web/graphic design, marketing, advertising, or a combination of these fields. Yet, not everyone who is a grow master has a degree in agriculture. Some have degrees in science, business, or marketing, but learned their skills on the job.

In the United States, only one traditional college—Northern Michigan University—offers a marijuana-related major. It recently began offering a Medicinal Plant Chemistry bachelor's degree for those who want to work in the cannabis, herbal extract, and natural product industries. Students in this program take classes such as General Chemistry, Organic Chemistry, Biochemistry, Medicinal Plant Chemistry Seminar, Biology, Plant Physiology, Physical Geography, and Soil Science. They also can choose to pursue an Entrepreneurial (for aspiring business owners) or Bio-analytical Track (for those who like science) within the major.

Many marijuana industry workers have college degrees. Since few colleges grant degrees in marijuana-related areas, you should major in the area of the industry that you're interested in—agriculture, business management, science, or other fields.

Those in the Entrepreneurial Track also take the following courses:

- Principles of Accounting
- Entrepreneurship
- Financial Management
- New Venture Finance: Capital Formation and Legal Issues
- Introduction to Marketing
- Marketing for Entrepreneurship

In the Bio-Analytical Track, students also take the following classes:

- Chemistry of the Elements
- Chemical Equilibrium
- Atomic Spectrometry
- Introduction to Cell and Molecular Biology
- Genetics
- Biostatistics
- Boreal Flora

Some schools have been founded that focus solely on preparing students to work in the marijuana industry. Their quality of instruction varies greatly. It's a good idea to do a lot of research regarding the quality of classes and instructors. You should also check on the percentage of students who land jobs in the marijuana industry after graduation. If graduates of the school can't get jobs in the marijuana industry, it's probably not a good school.

Learn more about Oaksterdam University:

Oaksterdam University was founded in 2007 in Oakland, California. It bills itself as "America's first cannabis college," and it has about 30,000 alumni from more than thirty countries. The university has two departments: Business and Horticulture. It awards certificates to those who complete the program.

- Students in the **Business Program** (also called The Classic Program) learn about business, history, law, economics, and science as they relate to the marijuana industry. In the advanced section of the program, students learn how to start and run a compliant cannabis business (one that follows government rules about owning a business); and how to obtain, grade (determine the quality), and present marijuana products for sale. It also focuses on issues such as security, banking, taxes, and intellectual property (creative work or ideas that are protected by law). Classes in this program include Budtender and Patient Relations, Dispensary and Business Operations, Science of Cannabis, and Grow Demonstration.

- Students in the **Horticulture Program** participate in both classroom lectures and hands-on lab work with plants in all stages of development. They take classes such as Horticulture 101: Growing Safely and Responsibly; Anatomy and Physiology of the Cannabis Plant; Irrigation Systems; and Lab: Manicuring, Drying and Curing.

Which Educational Path is Best for Me?

Many people ask themselves this question, but there is no correct answer. You should pick the training option that is the best match for your personality, learning style, and employment goals. Here's a breakdown of your options and their pros and cons:

College

Pros: Most marijuana industry workers have a college degree, but it doesn't have to be cannabis-related. Having a degree will increase your chances of landing a job.

Cons: Training lasts from two to four years (or more, depending on the job), and you must pay tuition.

A Good Fit: For those who like a structured environment that combines both classroom and hands-on training.

Apprenticeship

Pros: Allows you to learn while you earn, and possibly get your foot in the door at an employer. You make money while you work (unlike college), but the pay is usually not very good. Note: some apprenticeships are unpaid.

Con: Cannabis industry apprenticeships are typically informal and not approved/run by unions or trade associations, so program quality varies greatly.

A Good Fit: For those who want to enter the workforce more quickly.

Informal Training

Pros: Allows you to get to work right away and receive a salary.

Cons: Training will not be as detailed as what you receive in a certificate or degree program. Such positions may not be a path to advancement.

A Good Fit: For those who do not need a structured educational setting to learn, and who are able to pick up their skills and knowledge on the job.

Working in Another Industry First

Pros: Developing your marketing, agriculture, accounting, business management, or other skills and experience in another industry will make you a more in-demand job candidate if you decide to work in the marijuana industry.

Con: Working in another industry will not give you specific cannabis-related training. As a result, it may be harder to get a job.

A Good Fit: For those who want to develop a wider range of skills and experiences, so they can work in a variety of industries, not just the cannabis industry.

Other schools to check out include The Grow School, Humboldt Cannabis College, Clover Leaf University, and Trichome Institute in the United States, and Cannabis College in The Netherlands.

Informal Training Opportunities

Some people learn their skills by simply getting a job at a cannabis dispensary, a grow operation, or other marijuana industry employer. At a dispensary, you'll start out as a cashier or stock clerk. Gradually, you'll obtain experience (and take some cannabis courses) and have the chance, at some stores, to become a budtender or assistant manager. Perhaps you'll eventually open your own dispensary. At a grow operation, you'll start out as a laborer, carrying supplies and tools, weeding, cleaning up, and performing other basic tasks. Eventually, you'll learn the ins and outs of marijuana planting, tending, and harvesting, and you could become a grow master.

Getting a Job

There are many ways to land a job in the marijuana industry. For most jobs, you'll need to be at least eighteen years of age. When you get to college, your school's career services office can help with job leads, or you might get a job offer after participating in an internship or apprenticeship. You could also simply contact marijuana farms, dispensaries, or other businesses to see what job opportunities are available. Still others work with recruiters, who match people who want a job with companies that need workers. Since many people want to enter the field, the key is to show enthusiasm for the field and a willingness to work hard. You don't have to use marijuana to get a job in the industry. You just need to show an interest in, a basic knowledge of, and enthusiasm for marijuana.

Although you may not be looking for a job just yet, many of these suggestions also provide good ways to learn more about education and careers in the field. Here are some popular job-search strategies:

Networking. Most jobs are filled via networking. In networking, you just tell as many people as possible that you are looking for a job. You also discuss job openings and good employers, and help others who are looking for a job. You have two networks. Your personal network consists of your friends and family. Your professional network consists of the following types of people:

Networking is a great source of job leads.

Salaries for Farmers and Agricultural Managers in Select U.S. States Where Cannabis is Legal

Florida: $106,020	Washington (B): $79,790
Pennsylvania: $87,000	New York: $75,360
Arkansas: $86,200	Illinois: $69,190
Ohio: $83,260	Michigan: $66,040
New Jersey: $82,050	Louisiana: $63,850
Arizona: $81,200	Oregon (B): $54,280
Minnesota: $80,500	New Mexico: $46,670
California (B): $80,170	

Source: U.S. Department of Labor

(Note: Only medical cannabis is legal in the states above except for those marked "B," for both medical and recreational use.)

- Classmates
- Teachers
- People you meet at marijuana industry events such as career fairs, seminars, and conferences
- People you meet online, including at social networking sites such as LinkedIn

It's never too early to begin building your network. You never know who might be able to give you advice on a good marijuana school or help you to find a job.

Job Boards. Jobs can be discovered by checking out internet job boards that allow users to search by job type, employer name, geographic region, salary, and other criteria. Here are a few popular cannabis industry job boards, as well as general job boards. Although you're not ready to look for a job yet, checking out job boards can teach you more about specific marijuana careers and the industry as a whole.

- http://directory.womengrow.com/jobs
- https://www.vangsters.com
- http://420careers.com
- http://www.weedhire.com
- https://www.indeed.com
- https://www.monster.com
- https://www.glassdoor.com
- https://www.linkedin.com

Unions and Professional Associations. Most workers in the marijuana industry are not members of unions, but union membership is increasing. Those who are members of unions often have a better chance of landing a job. They often receive higher pay and better benefits than those who are not members of unions. The United Food and Commercial Workers International Union (UFCW) represents cannabis professionals who work in growing and cultivating facilities, manufacturing and processing facilities, and laboratories and dispensaries in the United States and Canada. Its Cannabis Workers Rising campaign seeks to increase the level of professionalism in the medical marijuana industry. Budtenders United is a UFCW subgroup that encourages budtenders to join the union. Some cannabis workers are members of the International Brotherhood of Teamsters, which represents workers in the U.S. and Canada.

Professional associations offer many useful resources such as membership, networking events, training opportunities, and certification (a professional title earned by completing additional education, tests, and other requirements). Major cannabis-related associations include the Canadian Medical Cannabis Industry Association, Cannabis Canada Association, Cannabis Growers of Canada, Hemp Industries Association, Marijuana Business Association, Medical Marijuana Association, National Cannabis Industry Association, United States Cannabis Coalition, and Women Grow. Some industry associations have subdivisions or groups for cannabis workers. For example, the American Chemical Society has a Cannabis Chemistry Subdivision.

Chemists are in strong demand in the marijuana industry.

How Much Can I Earn?

Money is not the most important thing in life. Good health, a happy family life, and finding a career that is personally rewarding rank higher. On the other hand, it's important to learn what type of jobs pay what salaries so that you can make a career choice that matches your life goals.

Salaries for marijuana industry workers vary greatly based on their job title. For example, low-skilled agriculture workers make minimum wage (the minimum amount that a worker can be paid by law). Dispensary owners, cannabis lawyers, and cannabis consultants can earn $100,000 or more a year. Salaries also vary by level of experience, educational background, and location. Members of unions receive **fringe benefits** such as medical insurance, a pension, and other benefits. Some dispensaries, grow farms, and other employers also offer fringe benefits to full-time workers. If you own a dispensary or growing facility, you'll have to provide your own benefits.

Many people are employed in the agriculture sector of the industry. Marijuana growers in the United States earn average salaries of $32,094, according to PayScale. com. Earnings range from $24,876 to $72,943. CannabisTrainingUniversity.com reports that some marijuana growers can earn $1 million or more a year.

Dispensary owners can earn $100,000 to $1 million or more depending on the size of their facility and the number of clients served. Dispensary managers earn salaries that range from $70,000 to $100,000 or more.

Here are some salary ranges based on job listings for various marijuana careers and the state where the job was located, according to Leafly.com, Forbes, and PayScale. com:

- Analytical Chemist/Production Manager: $80,000 to $100,000 (Oregon)
- Budtender: $31,200 to $37,440 (California)
- Bud Trimmer: $24,960 to $31,200 (Nevada, California, Washington)
- Cannabis Edibles Facility Manager: $60,000 to $100,000 (various states)
- Edibles Chef: $40,000 to $100,000 (various states)
- Extraction Technician: $75,000 to $125,000 (various states)
- Fertilizer and Soil Sales and Marketing Professional: $40,000 to $60,000 (Oregon)
- Liquor and Cannabis Enforcement Officer: $50,000 to $60,000 (Washington)
- Sales/Marketing/Social Media Manager: $20,000 to $40,000 (Oregon)

1. What high school classes should you take to prepare to become a scientist in the marijuana industry?
2. What are the pros and cons of training via an apprenticeship?
3. How much can a marijuana industry worker earn?

research project

Talk to marijuana workers who trained for the field in different ways (college, apprenticeship, on-the-job training). Ask them the following questions: How long did the training take, and what did it involve? What did you like and dislike about this type of training? If given the chance, would you train the same way? What advice would you give to a young person regarding training to enter the field? Prepare a report that summarizes the interviews. Try to determine what would be the best training approach for you.

Working in a retail store while you're in high school will help you to develop the professionalism and customer service skills that you will need if you choose to work in a marijuana dispensary.

words to understand

alumni: Graduates of a school—often a college or university.

cannabis strains: Varieties of cannabis plants that are developed to have different properties and potencies.

hypothesis: An educated guess regarding a problem; it is the starting point for more investigation.

irrigation system: A mechanical system that supplies water to crops.

payroll: Money paid out by a business or other organization to employees in exchange for work that is completed.

stigma: Negative and unfair beliefs that people have about a person, organization, or object.

chapter 4

Key Skills and Methods of Exploration

Key Skills for Success

There are dozens of careers in the marijuana industry. Opportunities range from grow masters and cultivation technicians, to dispensary owners and budtenders, to edibles chefs and extraction technicians. Some jobs involve working with your hands and having a "green thumb," while others require communication and problem-solving skills. Here are some of the most important traits for marijuana workers. Remember, many of these skills are useful for all marijuana workers.

- **Customer-service skills.** Budtenders and other dispensary staff need excellent customer-service skills (communication, listening, friendliness, patience, etc.) to effectively explain various marijuana products. They need to know the difference between different **cannabis strains**, and how they interact with the human body. They know what type of marijuana product to suggest to customers with pain or inflammation, and what type to suggest for those who have epilepsy or cancer. Many new medical cannabis customers do not know much about marijuana, and dispensary workers need to patiently walk them through the process of choosing and buyng the right products.

Bud trimmers need good hand-eye coordination to use clippers effectively.

- **Professionalism.** The use of marijuana has been a bit of a joke for many people thanks to negative and/or silly depictions of marijuana smokers in movies, television shows, and books. The discovery of medical benefits of using marijuana has created new views of marijuana by the public. Yet, the **stigma** of the goofy pot smoker still exists. That's why it's very important that marijuana workers present themselves professionally to customers, government officials, and the public. They should dress professionally if they work with the public or in other business settings. They should also talk about marijuana in a serious manner so that people take them and their industry seriously.

- **Passion.** Many people view working in the marijuana industry as not just a job that pays the bills, but as a calling. They are passionate about the benefits of marijuana, and they want to tell others about its medical and recreational benefits. They are excited about being in this industry because it's interesting and new, and because it offers so many possibilities. Workers who are passionate about their jobs often get promoted, and being passionate about your career makes work a lot more fun.

- **Manual dexterity/good physical shape/mechanical skills.** Bud trimmers need good hand-eye coordination to use clippers effectively. If you work as a grow master, or a trades worker at a marijuana farm or grow facility, you'll need to be in good physical condition and be able to use tools and equipment to build and repair growing facilities. Knowledge of electrical and **irrigation system** setup and repair will come in handy if you work as a grow master.

- **Detail-oriented personality.** Details are important in the marijuana industry. For example, if a marijuana farmer fails to correctly set up a lighting or irrigation system, he or she could have a bunch of dead plants. If a dispensary manager doesn't keep track of inventory, he or she may run out of stock. If a scientist fails to properly record research findings, the results of a study might have to be thrown out.

- **Ability to work independently.** Whether you're working in the fields, in a dispensary, or on the road between sales calls, there will be plenty of time when you're on your own. As a result, you need to be a good time manager, be able to follow instructions without supervision, and work hard and not "goof off" when your manager is not around.

- **Teamwork skills.** Today's workplace features people from many different ethnic, occupational, and educational backgrounds, so you'll need to learn to get along with others and work as part of a team.

- **Business and computer skills.** To be a successful business owner and manager, you'll need to be good at managing staff, overseeing budgets, planning **payroll**, accounting, marketing (including on social media), and performing many other duties that keep your business operating successfully.

Exploring Career Opportunities in the Marijuana Industry as a Student

While you certainly shouldn't use marijuana unless you're an adult (or unless you have a medical condition and permission from your doctor and parents), there are many other ways to learn more about marijuana and careers in the field. Here are some methods to explore:

Take Some Classes. The marijuana industry offers many career options, so middle school and high school can give you a good general introduction to the types of topics you'll need to know about if you pursue a marijuana career.

For example, if you plan to open your own dispensary or own or manage a farm, you should take business, accounting, finance, and related classes. If you want to be a chemist, research scientist, or lab technician, you should take biology, molecular biology, earth science, genetics, and chemistry classes. Lab courses will give you hands-on experience conducting experiments and testing your **hypotheses** about challenges in science. If you want to build and maintain marijuana growing areas and facilities, you should take shop/vocational tech classes. Other useful classes include English, speech, foreign languages, mathematics, computer science, art/design, and physics.

Molecular biology, earth science, genetics, chemistry, and other science classes will come in handy if you want to be a chemist, research scientist, or lab technician.

Some high schools offer specialized programs in agriculture. These programs will help you to prepare to become a grow master or work in other agricultural jobs. You'll get hands-on experience growing a wide range of fruits and vegetables (but not marijuana). At many schools, students get to select an agriculture-related pathway based on their interests. Pathways include:

- Agricultural Finance and Economics
- Agricultural Mechanics and Technology
- Animal Science
- Food Science and Technology
- Horticulture
- Biotechnology in Agriculture

Join an Association or School Club

Many countries have agricultural associations that you can join to learn more about agricultural careers. For example, the National FFA Organization (https://www.ffa.org) offers career resources and a lot of fun activities for young people in the United States. The National FFA Organization used to be called "Future Farmers of America," but it changed its name to reach out to people who are interested in other agriculture careers. Its members are preparing for careers in chemistry, agribusiness, agrimarketing, science, communications, education, horticulture, veterinary science, production, natural resources, forestry, and other fields. Another popular organization is 4-H (https://4-h.org), where you will complete hands-on projects in areas such as agriculture, health, science, and citizenship.

Other countries also offer similar clubs. For example, there are more than one hundred TeenAg Clubs (http://www.teenag.co.nz/clubs) in New Zealand. The National Federation of Young Farmers' Clubs (http://www.nfyfc.org.uk) provides opportunities in the United Kingdom. Junior Farmers' Association of Ontario and 4-H Canada offer good opportunities for young people in Canada.

If you're more interested in the business side of the marijuana industry, consider joining Future Business Leaders of America-Phi Beta Lambda, Inc. (http://www.fbla-pbl.org). This U.S. organization for junior high, middle school, high school, and college students offers academic competitions, leadership development opportunities, and educational programs that will teach you more about business and career paths. There are also science clubs for young people.

The National FFA Organization, 4-H, and other youth associations often work with middle schools and high schools to offer agriculture-related programs. Ask your school counselor for information on programs at your school. No agriculture, business, or science clubs at your school? Then start one with your classmates!

Learn why it's a good idea to join the National FFA Organization:

Participate in an Information Interview or Job Shadowing Experience. When you hear the phrase "information interview," you might think you're asking for a job. But that's not the case. In this type of interview, you're just talking with a marijuana industry worker about his or her job. These types of interviews, which can be done on the phone or in-person, are also a good way to meet people in the marijuana industry. You'll find that most people like to talk about their careers. Here are some questions to ask during the interview:

- Can you tell me about a day in your life on the job?
- What's your work environment like? Do you have to travel for your job?
- What are the most important personal and professional qualities for people in your career?
- What do you like best and least about your career?
- What is the future employment outlook for people in your career? How is the field changing?

- What can I do now to prepare for the field (classes, activities, projects, etc.)?

Job shadowing is another way to learn about marijuana careers. You'll follow a worker around for a few hours or an entire day to see what his or her job is like. You'll need to be at least eighteen (twenty-one in some areas) to visit a marijuana dispensary or farm. But, if you're younger, you could visit a marketing or law firm that provides services to the marijuana industry, or perhaps a laboratory. Visiting a traditional farm and job shadowing a farmer will give you a similar overview to the duties of a grow master.

Ask your parents, teachers, or school counselors to help arrange information interviews or job shadowing experiences.

When you turn twenty-one, you can tour a marijuana farm or dispensary. Many marijuana businesses offer tours to educate the public about the process or growing and selling marijuana. If you're not twenty-one, check out some tours of marijuana farms and grow facilities at YouTube.com

Tour a state-of-the-art indoor marijuana grow facility:

Plant a Garden. One of the best ways to learn more about agriculture is to get your hands dirty and plant, care for, and harvest crops. It's rewarding to grow fruit or vegetable plants from seed or tiny plant to a full-sized plant. Plus, it's fun to eat the products of your hard work. Marijuana should not be on your list of plants to grow, but try growing some peppers, tomatoes, beans, and other fruits and vegetables. YouTube is an excellent source of how-to videos. The following books also offer good ideas:

Any experience you can obtain gardening will give you a head-start when it comes time to learn how to grow cannabis.

- *Vegetable Gardening For Dummies*, by The Editors of the National Gardening Association and Charlie Nardozzi (For Dummies, 2009)
- *A Teen Guide to Eco-Gardening*, Food, and Cooking, by Jen Green (Heinemann, 2013)
- *Beginner's Illustrated Guide to Gardening: Techniques to Help You Get Started*, by Katie Elzer-Peters (Cool Springs Press, 2012)
- *Kitchen Gardening for Beginners*, by Simon Akeroyd (DK, 2013)

Visit the Websites of Marijuana Colleges. Many people prepare for careers in this field by earning certificates and degrees in marijuana-related topics. It's a good idea to visit the websites of these schools to learn more about typical classes, watch videos of students in classes and laboratories, and learn more about schools so you can make a good choice when it comes time to attend college. Many schools offer tours so future students can see the campus and meet professors. In the United States, only one traditional college—Northern Michigan University—offers a marijuana-related major. It offers a medicinal plant chemistry bachelor's degree for those who want to work in the cannabis, herbal extract, and natural product industries. Oaksterdam University bills itself as "America's first cannabis college." The university was founded in 2007 in Oakland, California. It has about 30,000 **alumni** from more than thirty countries. The university has two departments: Business and Horticulture.

Contact the following organizations for more information on education and careers in the marijuana industry:

American Chemical Society
Cannabis Chemistry Subdivision
http://www.dchas.org/cann

Australian Cannabis Industry Association
http://www.australiancannabisindustry.org

Cannabis Canada Association
http://www.cann-can.ca

Hemp Industries Association
https://thehia.org

Marijuana Business Association
http://mjba.net

Medical Marijuana Association
http://www.medicinalmarijuanaassociation.com

National Cannabis Industry Association
https://thecannabisindustry.org

Women Grow
https://womengrow.com

You can learn more by visiting https://oaksterdamuniversity.com. Perhaps one of its professors would be willing to participate in an information interview about education and careers in the field. Here are some other schools to check out:

- The Grow School (United States): http://www.thegrowschool.org
- Humboldt Cannabis College (United States): http://707humboldtcannabiscollege.com
- Clover Leaf University (United States): http://cloverleafuniversity.com

Touring a marijuana dispensary will provide an excellent introduction to careers at dispensaries. But you will need to be at least age eighteen to do so.

- Northeastern Institute of Cannabis (United States): https://instituteofcannabis.com
- Trichome Institute (United States): https://www.trichomeinstitute.com
- Cannabis College (The Netherlands): http://www.cannabiscollege.com

text-dependent questions

1. How do marijuana industry workers use their communication skills?
2. Why is professionalism so important to marijuana workers?
3. What are two ways to explore marijuana careers as a student?

research project

Try at least three of the suggestions in this chapter (clubs, information interviewing, etc.) to explore the field. Write a report detailing what you learned. What is the best method of exploration, and why?

Sixty percent of Americans surveyed in 2016 believed that cannabis should be legalized.

words to understand

decriminalize: To reduce or get rid of punishments for the possession and use of small amounts of cannabis.

economy: Activities related to the production, use, and trade of services and goods in a city, state, region, or country.

opioid abuse crisis: The serious misuse of prescription opioids and the use of heroin, an illegal drug, which can result in injury and death. More than six out of ten drug overdoses in the U.S. are opioid-related.

post-traumatic stress disorder: A mental health condition that is experienced by some military veterans; those who have been victims of natural disasters, serious accidents, terrorist incidents, or physical or sexual assault; and others.

revenue: Money that is earned from the sale of products or services before expenses are subtracted.

chapter 5

The Future of Careers in the Marijuana Industry

The Big Picture

It's a good time to pursue a career in the marijuana industry. Changing attitudes toward the use of medical marijuana and, to a lesser extent, recreational marijuana, are creating strong job growth in the marijuana industry in some countries. Here are some stats that support this trend:

- Sixty percent of Americans surveyed in 2016 believed that cannabis should be legalized. This was a big increase from the 25 percent of Americans who believed so in 1980. (Gallup)

- In 2017, 51 percent of Canadians reported that they were in favor of legalization. Thirty-three percent were against legalization, and 14 percent neither favored nor were against the measure. (NRG Research Group)

- In 2016, 29 percent of Mexicans favored cannabis legalization—an increase of 21 percent from a decade earlier. (Parametría)

Approximately 165,000 to 230,000 full- and part-time workers are employed in the U.S. cannabis industry.

Scientists have done research that shows that cannabis can be used to treat pain, nausea caused by cancer and other diseases, poor appetite and weight loss caused by chronic illnesses, seizure disorders, and other medical conditions. Cannabis is also being used to help fight the **opioid abuse crisis** and **post-traumatic stress disorder**. Countries that have legalized medical cannabis in recent years include parts of the United States, Canada, Australia, Spain, Portugal, The Netherlands, Jamaica, Colombia, the Czech Republic, Switzerland, Romania, Germany, India, Israel, Macedonia, South Africa, and Uruguay.

A small, but growing number of countries, have also legalized or **decriminalized** the use of recreational cannabis by adults. Recreational use of cannabis has been decriminalized in some U.S. states, the United Kingdom, Ireland, France, Denmark, Italy, Spain, Czech Republic, and Germany, although it is still technically illegal. The Netherlands has long ignored recreational cannabis use, but has recently created stricter laws.

Growing Opportunities in the United States

In the United States, most states allow the use of medical marijuana, although some states do not allow marijuana to be grown in the state. Additionally, eight states have legalized recreational cannabis for adult use: Alaska, California, Colorado, Maine, Massachusetts, Nevada, Oregon, and Washington.

In 2017, 51 percent of Canadians reported that they favored the legalization of marijuana.

Did You Know?

- In 2017, 52 percent of U.S. adults had used cannabis in some shape or form, and, of those, 44 percent still used cannabis. (Yahoo News/Marist Poll)

- About 21 percent of the U.S. population lives in a state where using marijuana is legal. (MarketWatch.com)

- About 147 million people, or 2.5 percent of the world population, use cannabis annually. That is more than the percentage who use opiates (.2 percent) and cocaine (.2 percent) combined. (World Health Organization)

Revenues in the U.S. legal cannabis market alone were $6.6 billion in 2016, according to a report from New Frontier Data.

The U.S. cannabis industry employs 165,000 to 230,000 full and part-time (often on the grow side of the business) workers. This includes those who directly handle cannabis, and those who work at companies that earn a large amount of revenue from providing services to the marijuana industry. It's estimated that the legal cannabis market will create more than 250,000 new jobs within three years. This is higher than the expected new jobs that will become available in manufacturing, utilities (electricity, natural gas, water, etc.), or the government. The employment data "shows that the [marijuana] industry is becoming an economic engine for the country," according to Chris Walsh, the editorial director of *Marijuana Business Daily*. Demand is strong for store managers, budtenders, and chefs and others with food production experience.

Marijuana Business Daily says that "infused products and edibles are the fastest-growing category in the cannabis industry, proving extremely popular with recreational consumers and medical patients alike." It also says that companies that provide support services (accounting, marketing, etc.) to the cannabis industry are "generating excellent returns."

In addition to careers that are specific to the marijuana industry—such as budtender, extraction technician, and grow master—it takes many other workers to make the

A scientist studies marijuana on a farm. Demand for scientists in the marijuana industry is expected to be strong during the next decade.

industry successful. For example, accountants, chief financial officers, and financial clerks help businesses keep financial records and follow government financial rules. Lawyers provide legal advice to cannabis farm and dispensary owners. Security workers check customers' identification and protect dispensaries from theft, and drivers transport cannabis and cannabis-infused products from farms and laboratories to dispensaries, medical facilities, and other locations. Construction and trades workers (such as carpenters, electricians, and heating and cooling technicians) are needed to build, repair, and maintain growing facilities and equipment. Governments employ inspectors to make sure that marijuana farms, dispensaries, and laboratories follow the law. In short, there are a lot of options to explore before you make a career choice. Here are job growth predictions for some of these careers. It's important to remember that job demand varies by state. Also, employment growth may change by the time you enter the workforce. Projections are made for the next decade.

- Accountants: +10 percent, faster than the average for all careers
- Carpenters: +8 percent, as fast as the average
- Chemists: +7 percent, as fast as the average
- Chief financial officers: +19 percent, much faster than the average

- Electricians: +9 percent, as fast as the average
- Geneticists: +11 percent, faster than the average
- Inspectors (agricultural): +5 percent, as fast as the average
- Laboratory technicians: +4 percent, slower than the average
- Lawyers: +9 percent, as fast as the average
- Marketing managers: +10 percent, faster than the average
- Plant scientists: +9 percent, as fast as the average
- Software developers: +24 percent, much faster than the average

Did You Know?

Forbes projects that the international market for non-psycho-active hemp oil (known as cannabidiol, or CBD) could grow by 700 percent by 2020.

Budding Opportunities Outside the United States

While many countries have legalized medical marijuana or decriminalized the use of recreational marijuana, it's against the law to grow marijuana in some of these countries. As a result, there are not a lot of marijuana workers in countries that don't have cannabis growing facilities. Canada and The Netherlands are expected to offer the best marijuana industry job prospects in coming years because they allow the growth of marijuana for export to other countries.

Canadian companies export marijuana to Germany (which many consider the most attractive European medical cannabis market), Croatia, Brazil, Chile, New Zealand, and other countries. Currently, there are only about forty-five licensed producers of medical cannabis in Canada. These companies generate $400 million annually in revenue and provide medical cannabis to 153,000 medical marijuana patients, according to the financial services firm Canaccord Genuity Group. Once recreational cannabis becomes legal, the number of recreational users could increase to four million by 2021, and the combined medical/recreational market in Canada could reach $8 billion a year. It is estimated that 150,000 new cannabis jobs will be created in Canada during the next few years. Industry experts predict that demand will be especially strong for workers in cultivation, accounting, and marketing.

Companies in The Netherlands ship marijuana to Australia, Canada, and European Union countries such as Germany, Italy, and Finland. The types of cannabis exports include the entire flower, CBD oil, and cannabinoid-based liquid capsules.

Israel is a capital of medical marijuana research, but it does not ship marijuana outside of its borders. Germany recently legalized the use of medical marijuana, but it does not grow much marijuana in-country. It plans to increase marijuana growing in-country soon.

Learn more about the all-female work crew at High Gorgeous, which makes canna-bis-infused beauty products:

Challenges to Employment Growth

The marijuana industry continues to experience strong growth in many countries around the world. Despite this positive outlook, some developments could negatively affect the industry.

Growth will slow if, for some reason, public opinion about the use of medical or recreational marijuana reverses toward prohibition (not allowing people to use it) or if stricter laws are passed. For example, if voters in individual states or countries push for a return to prohibition, marijuana businesses may be forced to close.

Women in the Marijuana Industry

Women play a major role in the marijuana industry—working in jobs that range from grow master, to budtender, to cannabis business owner. In fact, women are majority owners in 57 percent of cannabis businesses, according to New Frontier Data. In the entire industry, women hold 26 percent of leadership positions, according to a survey of cannabis executives and professionals by *Marijuana Business Daily*. That's higher than the 20 percent average for women leaders in all U.S. companies. Female leadership rates were even higher (although some were lower) in certain marijuana industry sectors:

- Ancillary services firms (law firms, marketing agencies, etc.): 43 percent
- Testing labs: 33 percent
- Medical or recreational retailers: 26 percent
- Infused products makers: 25 percent
- Wholesale cultivation: 22 percent

Organizations such as Women Grow (https://womengrow.com), which was launched in 2014, provide networking opportunities for women and make sure that they continue to play a big role in the industry. The organization (which is open to both women and men) offers monthly events in more than thirty-five cities in the United States and Canada.

If medical research determines that there are more negative or potentially dangerous side effects that occur after using marijuana, the public may be less willing to use marijuana for recreational or medical purposes. In this instance, governments might change laws to prohibit or severely limit the use of cannabis. This would negatively affect the industry.

Although many U.S. states have legalized the use of recreational and/or medical marijuana, the use of cannabis is still illegal at the federal level.

Marijuana businesses remain very concerned about the possibility of intervention by the federal government. In the United States, the commercial growing of medical and recreational marijuana is technically illegal. In the past, the federal government has said that it would allow states to make and enforce their own laws regarding marijuana growing and sales. Government attitudes may change based on the political party that is in power. If a political party that is against the use of cannabis is in power, it may enforce more stringent laws and penalties. It could even shut down marijuana farms and dispensaries that produce and sell recreational marijuana—eliminating jobs and the entire industry. In 2017, cannabis businesses said that the threat of federal intervention to their businesses was the number one challenge to being successful, according to *Marijuana Business Daily*.

The growth of the marijuana industry may slow if the **economy** weakens and another recession (a period of significant economic decline) occurs. People will have less money to spend on recreational marijuana, and some farms and dispensaries might close. Large tax revenues in states that have legalized cannabis will decline. The sale of medical marijuana may also decline because its cost is not currently covered by health insurance. If a recession causes cannabis farms and dispensaries to close, businesses that provide support services (accounting, transportation, security, marketing, etc.) will also close or be forced to lay off employees. The recreational marijuana tourist industry will also decline if fewer people travel to legal states to use cannabis.

The marijuana industry may face challenges if the U.S. government or other countries fully legalize recreational and medical marijuana and tobacco companies begin to produce marijuana products. These companies have a long history of making cigarettes and related products inexpensively. They could use this knowledge to take business away from the marijuana industry.

Finally, it's important to remember that there is currently a shortage of qualified marijuana workers in some areas, but as more people learn about exciting career options in the industry, open jobs will be filled and competition for jobs will increase. But if more states and countries legalize recreational and medical marijuana, demand for cannabis will rise, which should also create more need for workers.

Did You Know?

Even though the use of cannabis is legal in many states, the U.S. government still classifies it as a Schedule 1 Drug (like LSD or heroin). These drugs are tightly regulated by the federal government because it considers them the most dangerous with a high potential for abuse and with no accepted medical use.

A Look Ahead

It's hard to predict the future of the marijuana industry because of the factors (laws, changing public opinion, competition from other industries, etc.) we just discussed. But if we take a positive viewpoint, the sky is the limit for the marijuana industry. If medical marijuana is legalized in more U.S. states and other countries, it will gradually become a part of the established health care industry. New types of health care workers—such as marijuana physician, marijuana nurse, and marijuana therapist—may emerge to help treat patients who can be helped by using marijuana. Demand will grow for specialized researchers to discover more positive medical benefits of marijuana, as well as investigate the negative side effects of its use. If more countries legalize recreational use, marijuana dispensaries may become as common as coffee shops. Demand will greatly increase for growers, marijuana dispensary workers, and others that help prepare, market, and sell cannabis. Government agencies will also need to create special enforcement divisions to monitor marijuana farms and dispensaries. This will create more jobs for inspectors and regulatory workers. These are all just educated guesses about the future. But the fast growth of the industry and increasing legalization suggests that at least some of these predictions will come true.

In Closing

Can you see yourself growing marijuana on a farm or in an indoor facility, explaining the merits of a type of cannabis to customers at a dispensary, managing the finances for a marijuana business, or creating an advertising campaign to convince people to buy marijuana edibles, oils, or other products? Do you like helping people to improve their health? Do you like good pay and a chance to get in on the ground floor of a fast-growing industry? If you answered "yes" to all these questions, then a rewarding career in the marijuana industry could be in your future. I hope that you'll use this book as a starting point to learn about the many career paths in the marijuana industry. Talk to budtenders, dispensary owners, cannabis industry lawyers, and others about their careers and shadow them on the job, use the resources of professional organizations and unions, and try your hand at basic gardening to learn more about the agricultural aspects of the field and build your skills. Good luck on your career exploration!

New types of health care workers—such as marijuana physician, marijuana nurse, and marijuana therapist—may emerge to help treat patients who can be helped by using cannabis.

Did You Know?

Some countries still have very restrictive laws regarding the use of cannabis. These nations include China, France, Nigeria, Norway, Poland, Ukraine, the Philippines, Singapore, Japan, Vietnam, Malaysia, Indonesia, South Korea, Thailand, Saudi Arabia, the United Arab Emirates, and Turkey.

text-dependent questions

1. How many people work in the U.S. marijuana industry? How many jobs are expected to be added in the next several years?
2. What is the status of the marijuana industry in Canada?
3. What are some developments that might slow employment for workers in the marijuana industry?

research project

Ask your friends and neighbors if they think medical and recreational marijuana should be legalized, and why? What are the main reasons that they provide for and against legalization? What is your opinion about the legalization of marijuana? Write a report that summarizes your opinions and those of your friends and neighbors and present it to your class.

adult-use cannabis: The recreational use of cannabis by those over the age of twenty-one.

cannabidiol (CBD): A chemical compound found in the cannabis plant that is non-psychoactive. It is known for its medical and pain relief properties.

cannabinoid: Any of various chemical compounds (such as THC) from the cannabis or marijuana plant that produces a euphoric feeling, or "high."

cannabis clubs: Marijuana growing and consumption cooperatives (a group that is owned and run by its members) that exist in countries such as Uruguay and Spain to provide cannabis users with marijuana products and a place to use those products.

cannabis strains: Varieties of cannabis plants that are developed to have different properties and potencies.

clinical trials: Experiments with unproven medications that may or may not help a patient get better.

dabbing: A somewhat controversial method of cannabis flash-vaporization. It has very strong effects on the user.

decriminalization: The legal term for getting rid of or reducing criminal charges for having or using cannabis.

delta-9-tetrahydrocannabinol (THC): A natural chemical compound found in the flowers of the marijuana plant. It produces a feeling of euphoria and a psychoactive reaction, or "high," when marijuana is eaten or smoked.

dopamine: A naturally occurring chemical in the human body that increases pleasurable feelings in the mind and body.

drug trafficking: A global illegal trade involving the growth, manufacture, distribution, and sale of substances, such as cannabis, that are subject to drug prohibition laws.

edible: A food made or infused (cooked or otherwise prepared) with cannabis extracts (portions of the plant, including seeds or flowers).

endocannabinoid system: A group of cannabinoid receptors found in the brain and central and peripheral nervous systems of mammals that help control appetite, pain, mood, and memory.

euphoria: A feeling of intense well-being and happiness.

extracts: Portions of the marijuana plant, including seeds or flowers.

hash: A solid or resinous extract of cannabis.

hemp: A cannabis plant grown for its fiber and used to make rope, textiles, paper, and other products.

ingest: To take food, drink, or another substance into the body.

lethargy: Lack of enthusiasm and energy; a common side effect of cannabis use.

Marihuana Tax Act of 1937: A marijuana taxation act that led to the prohibition of cannabis in the United States during much of the twentieth century.

marijuana: A cannabis plant that is smoked or consumed as a psychoactive (mind-altering) drug.

marijuana dispensary: A place where people can buy recreational or medical cannabis. Dispensaries are tightly controlled by the government.

marijuana oil: Liquid that is extracted from the hemp plant and placed in either capsule form or combined with foods or drinks. CBD is most commonly consumed as an oil.

medical cannabis identification card: A document issued by a state where it is legal to use medical cannabis; the card indicates that a patient may use, buy, or have medical cannabis at home, on his or her person, or both.

neuroprotectant: A substance that repairs and protects the nervous system, its cells, structure, and function.

neurotransmitter: Chemicals that communicate information in the human body.

opiates: Substances derived from the opium poppy plant such as heroin.

opium: A highly addictive narcotic drug that is created by collecting and drying the milky juice that comes from the seed pods of the poppy plant.

prohibition: The action of forbidding something, especially by law.

propaganda: False information that is created to influence people.

prosecution: The conducting of legal proceedings against someone if it is believed that they broke the law.

psychoactive drug: A drug that affects the mind.

psychosis: Detachment from reality.

receptors: Groups of specialized cells that can convert energy into electrical impulses.

repeal: To get rid of a law or congressional act.

shatter: Cannabis concentrate that looks like colored glass.

social cannabis use: The use of cannabis in social settings, whether in public or private.

tar: A toxic byproduct of cigarette or marijuana smoking.

tincture: A medicine made by dissolving a drug in alcohol, vinegar, or glycerites.

topicals: Cannabis-infused lotions, balms, and salves that relieve pain and aches at the application site on the body.

vaporizer: A device that is used to turn water or medicated liquid into a vapor for inhalation.

War on Drugs: An anti-drug campaign started in the United States in 1971 by then-president Richard Nixon. Its goal was to fight drug abuse and shipments of illegal drugs to the U.S. from Latin America, Mexico, and other places.

Index

Photo Credits

Cover: Matrain | Dreamstime.com

Cover: Eric Limon | Dreamstime.com

Interior book cover: Alexander Raths | Dreamstime.com

7: Andreblais | Dreamstime.com

8: Andreblais | Dreamstime.com

10: Iphotothailand | Dreamstime.com

11: Buppha Wuttifery | Dreamstime

13: Ben Schonewille | Dreamstime.com

15: Radub85 | Dreamstime

17: Ekaterina79 | Dreamstime.com

18: Openrangestock | Dreamstime.com

19: Nathanphoto | Dreamstime.com

20: Peter Kim | Dreamstime.com Medical

24: Wavebreakmedia Ltd | Dreamstime.com

25: Dragonimages | Dreamstime

26: Elnur | Dreamstime.com

29: Michael Nosek | Dreamstime.com

31: Atomazul | Dreamstime

34: Monkey Business Images | Dreamstime

35: Iakov Filimonov | Dreamstime.com

37: Robert Kneschke | Dreamstime

40: Robert Kneschke | Dreamstime.com

44: Monkey Business Images | Dreamstime.com

47: Crazinero | Dreamstime.com

50: Ikonoklastfotografie | Dreamstime.com

51: Kyle Taisacan | Dreamstime.com

53: Monkey Business Images | Dreamstime

57: Spectral-design | Dreamstime.com

59: Smontgom65 | Dreamstime.com

60: Sarra22 | Dreamstime

61: Sborisov | Dreamstime.com

62: Nuvista | Dreamstime.com

64: Stokkete | Dreamstime.com

68: Matthew Benoit | Dreamstime.com

70: Carlos Restrepo | Dreamstime.com

Further Reading & Internet Resources

Blesching, Uwe. *The Cannabis Health Index: Combining the Science of Medical Marijuana with Mindfulness Techniques to Heal 100 Chronic Symptoms and Diseases.* Berkeley, Calif.: North Atlantic Books, 2015.

Goldsberry, Debby. *Starting & Running a Marijuana Business.* New York: Alpha, 2017.

Hageseth, Christian, and Joseph D'Agnese. *Big Weed: An Entrepreneur's High-Stakes Adventures in the Budding Legal Marijuana Business.* New York: St. Martin's Press, 2015.

Hudak, John. *Marijuana: A Short History.* Washington, D.C.: Brookings Institution Press, 2016.

Lee, Martin A. *Smoke Signals: A Social History of Marijuana: Medical, Recreational and Scientific.* New York: Scribner, 2013.

Internet Resources

https://www.drugabuse.gov/drugs-abuse/marijuana This is the official U.S. government website for marijuana created by the National Institute on Drug Abuse. It includes a description of marijuana and its health effects, as well as statistics and information on trends and research.

https://hightimes.com/business/high-times-top-13-marijuana-jobs This article from the marijuana publication *High Times* provides information on thirteen fast-growing careers in the cannabis industry, including budtender, edibles cook, and computer programmer.

https://www.cheatsheet.com/money-career/jobs-being-created-by-the-marijuana-industry.html/?a=viewall This website provides information on sixteen careers in the marijuana industry, including concentrates processor, trimmer, and farmer.

https://newfrontierdata.com/annualreport2017 Visit this website to download the executive summary of *The Cannabis Industry Annual Report*, from New Frontier Data. The summary features statistics about the North American legal cannabis market, survey results that detail the public's views on cannabis legalization, and information on how cannabis is being used to fight the opioid epidemic.

http://www.ncsl.org/research/health/state-medical-marijuana-laws.aspx This is the official website of the National Conference for State Legislatures. It provides information on current U.S. medical cannabis laws.

About the Author:

Andrew Morkes has been a writer and editor for more than 25 years. He is the author of more than 20 books about college-planning and careers, including many titles in this series, the *Vault Career Guide to Social Media*, and *They Teach That in College!?: A Resource Guide to More Than 100 Interesting College Majors*, which was selected as one of the best books of the year by the library journal *Voice of Youth Advocates*. He is also the author and publisher of "The Morkes Report: College and Career Planning Trends" blog.

Video Credits

Chapter 1:
Learn about the six main components of a female cannabis plant: http://x-qr.net/1HaT
A marijuana farmer discusses the rewards and challenges of owning a business: http://x-qr.net/1HME
Tour a marijuana-growing operation in Kasilof, Alaska, and see bud trimmers at work: http://x-qr.net/1EW1

Chapter 2:
Tour a medical marijuana dispensary, see what is required from a first-time visitor to a dispensary, and see a budtender at work.: http://x-qr.net/1Eth

Chapter 3:
Learn more about Oaksterdam University: http://x-qr.net/1Gjd

Chapter 4:
Learn why it's a good idea to join the National FFA Organization: http://x-qr.net/1FGT
Tour a state-of-the-art indoor marijuana grow facility: http://x-qr.net/1FLU

Chapter 5:
Learn more about the all-female work crew at High Gorgeous, which makes cannabis-infused beauty products: http://x-qr.net/1EGe